The Talk

Discussing Black America

By Dayson Brooks

THE TALK: DISCUSSING BLACK AMERICA

1405 SW 6th Avenue • Ocala, Florida 34471 • Phone 352-622-1825 • Fax 352-622-1875
Website: www.atlantic-pub.com • Email: sales@atlantic-pub.com
SAN Number: 268-1250

Library of Congress Control Number: 2020920260

Printed in the United States

PROJECT MANAGER: Jessie Ranew
INTERIOR LAYOUT AND JACKET DESIGN: Nicole Sturk

Preface

The phrase Black Lives Matter has become a symbol with both a polarizing and energizing effect. Some people consider this phrase and the movement behind it as exclusionary. They look at the Black Lives Matter movement and do not see any room for their own issues, and somehow conclude that Black Lives Matter means all lives don't; however, I see it the other way. I see Black Lives Matter as a movement that recognizes systemic racism, discrimination, inequality, and inequity, as well as police brutality, misconduct, and abuse. I see Black Lives Matter as a movement demanding change for those who have been crippled by American society and institutions, and I see Black Lives Matter as a movement that fights for my right to live as a black American. I wish it weren't, but this country has proven that a fight for black lives is incredibly necessary, which explains the importance of this book.

This book is a take on a conversation that is being had in black homes across the entire country. It's known as "The Talk," and it's a very important conversation that black parents have with their children about the weight their skin has in America. My book discusses the societal discrimination and victimization of black Americans, as well as the police brutality, misconduct, and abuse that has always been a stain on the values and ideology America is supposed to uphold. I wrote this book for three reasons: to teach black children how-to live-in America, to assist black parents in having this very difficult conversation with their children, and to give those who do not share black skin insight into the scary but necessary reality black parents must relay to their children. I want everyone who reads this book to understand the significance of its words, and I want everyone who reads this book to imagine the anger and fear that comes with telling your children how something that should be meaningless and insignificant ultimately determines the way the world treats you.

Mother: Von and Adria, we need to talk.

Adria: Talk about what?

Father: Well, baby girl, we need to tell you now how the world works for people like us.

Von: What do you mean?

Father: Black people, son. I know you two have seen the outrage from those in our community. I know you two have felt the anger, grief, and pain of all those screaming for change on the news, and I know you two have seen at least one of the countless videos where those who should protect and serve abuse their power.

Mother: This is why we need to talk. We need to tell you what our parents told us, and their parents told them.

Father: This talk has been passed down from generation to generation, and though years have passed, it has never lost its importance. For some reason, despite the progress made, the need to explain your skin and the danger that comes with it remains, so this is what you need to know.

The world sees you as both a commodity and a threat—something to use, yet fear. It accepts your music, your rhythm, your athletic abilities, and your talent, but it rejects your black skin, your curly hair, your swagger, and your finesse. This world looks at you and assumes that you must be up to no good.

Mother: Whether you are selling lemonade, having a barbecue in the park, taking a nap in the library, eating cereal on your own couch, taking a jog, or just trying to cash a check, you must be aware.

Father: You must be aware of the danger being black can bring to everything you do. You must never appear threatening because others will break you for it. Never get angry or loud because others do not understand your emotion, especially when it is coupled with your melanin.

Mother: And God, please never give the police any reason to stop you or even look at you because black and blue do not always mix. Our main objective is to come home safe and alive.

Von: But Mom, what if I don't give the police a reason to stop me, but they do it anyway?

Mother: Good question, son. As a black man, you may end up encountering police even without reason. So, if the police do stop you, do not talk back, do not look them in the eyes, do not make any sudden movements, and do not do what your white friends do because you are not like them. It's a shame to say, but even in this time and place, people view your skin differently, which means that no amount of intelligence, money, or influence will award you with the privileges white people have, and if something bad were to happen, neither your intelligence, money, or influence will provide you or us with the justice we deserve.

Von: So, what should I do?

Mother: Well son, I want you to comply with every demand the officer makes, record everything you can, and understand that, sadly, all the rights granted to you by this country have historically been ignored. Play it safe, focus on getting out of the situation, and remember that you are beautiful, loved, and needed.

Father: And baby girl, I want you to listen closely. Your struggles, unfortunately, will be just as great because you are both a woman and black, which is a combination that has been particularly burdened. However, you too are beautiful, loved, and needed.

Adria: Wait, Dad, what do you mean?

Father: Well, baby girl, your gender and skin color are looked down upon by society.

Mother: For example, women of color are paid less for completing the same job that a white man, a white woman, or even a black man might do. This means that if both you and your brother wash the dishes and clean your rooms at the same time, in the same way, your brother will still be given more money than you.

Adria: But that's not fair!

Mother: You're right—it's not fair. That's why we're having this conversation.

Father: This country has proven that life isn't fair over and over again for people that look like you and me.

Mother: And as hard as it is to have this talk, we, as your parents, have the responsibly to tell you just how unfair this world can be, so that you can be prepared for whatever life may bring.

Father: So, children, I want you to remember these names: Emmett Till, Trayvon Martin, Philando Castile, Tamir Rice, Freddie Gray, Eric Garner, Breonna Taylor, Botham Jean, Sandra Bland, Ahmaud Arbery, and George Floyd. I want you to remember that in this country horrible things happened to these people and many others solely based on the color of their skin. I want you to understand the harsh truth—you are no different and that with one wrong move you can end up in the same position as them, or in a jail cell. Unfortunately, this is the America we live in—it is a place known for being the home of the free and land of the brave, for being driven by justice and equality.

Mother: But children, I want you to remember that these American values do not always extend or apply to people who look like us.

Father: Evidence of this has been plastered across history and extends all the way back to the inception of this country. With all this being said, I do not want you to be scared, but I cannot blame you if you are because all this scares me too. My mom and dad gave me the same talk when I was a child, and the idea that I was seen as somehow different and had to act differently made me so angry. But I was also so afraid because the color of my skin was something I could not control although others treated me like it was. Now that I have kids of my own and have to relay the same information, I can't help but feel the same way—afraid and angry.

Mother: But the key is to be proactive in your fear—to mold your nightmares into dreams worth pursuing and to use your anger to fuel your pursuits.

Father: This talk was not only to warn you of the danger that comes with being black, but to also inspire you to one day remove that danger from the equation entirely.

Mother: We want you both to understand what we're saying; heed our warnings and use the information we give you to change the world for the better.

Adria: But how? How can we do that when everything seems to be against us?

Von: What hope do we have to fix what's broken?

Mother: How do we change this world for the better despite the institutions and systems kneeling on our throats? How do we finally win this 400-year race?

Father: We keep running. The only sure way to make change is to keep fighting for it, keep protesting, keep writing letters to public officials, keep speaking out, keep donating to important causes, keep learning, and most importantly, keep voting.

Mother: You may be too young to vote now, but voting is a very important part of our way of life, and by ignoring it, we're accepting all the wrong that comes our way.

Father: So, children, we'll leave you with this.

Mother: You are both the most important things in our lives and to our future, so it's incredibly important that you two recognize how this world views your blackness and act accordingly. It's also very important that you two find a way to change the way the world views your blackness. Make them see your beauty, intellect, and strength the same way we do. Make your voices heard and your struggle recognized, and make this county live up to the values and ideals it prides itself on.

Father: This is your charge, your quest, and your responsibility as our children and as proud black Americans.

Grow strong, live long, and make a world that no longer has any need for this talk.